"For Matthew Lees who is relentlessly positive."

STOP...THINK...CHOOSE...DO!
Make Good Consequences Happen For You!

St*op* • • T*h*i*nk* • • C*h*oose

***BEFORE* you DO**

to make good consequences

happen for you!

BEFORE you ask for trouble,

or give out looks that freeze...

BEFORE you whine or stomp your feet,
or hit or kick or tease …

BEFORE you say bad words,

or use words that sting...

BEFORE you sneak a cookie, or take your sister's things...

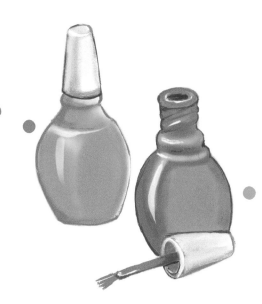

BEFORE you refuse to stay in bed,
or forget to do your chores...

BEFORE you throw a tantrum,
or slam your bedroom door...

BEFORE you pout and cry,

or complain that it's not fair...

St**o**p • • **T**h**i**n**k** • • **C**h**oo**s**e**

BEFORE you **DO**

to make good consequences
happen for you!

STOP

Don't even blink!

Give yourself
time to think!

Breathe slow and deep!

BEFORE you think,
don't utter a peep!

STOP

Walk away!
Cool down!

If you keep going,
this will end with your frown!

12

Stop • • **Think** • • **Choose**

BEFORE you **DO**

to make good consequences

happen for you!

Thinking is a talk
that you have
with YOU.
You ask yourself,
"What will I DO?"

Think

Who is involved?

What trouble am I in?

What can I do?

How can everyone win?

Think

What do I want to happen?

What is in the way?

What do I need to know?

What do I need to say?

How are others feeling?

How can I be a friend?

If I have hurt other's feelings,

how can I make amends?

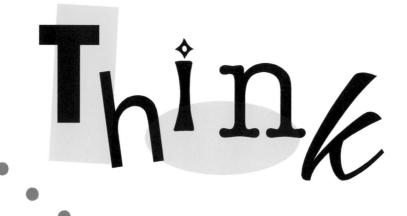

Is it helpful to keep asking
if I am told "no"?
Where do I want
this situation to go?

St**o**p • • **T**h**i**n**k** • • **C**h**oo**s**e**

BEFORE *you* **DO**

to make good consequences
happen for you!

Choosing is deciding which consequence to pursue.

Doing is the behavior
that you decide to do.

You Choose

Kinder?
or
Meaner?

If you CARE and SHARE,
a kinder world will be.

If you are "all about ME,"
a meaner world you will see!

You Choose

Friendship?
or
Lonely?

If you are COOPERATIVE,
you will keep your friends!

If you are BOSSY or GRUMPY,
you will be lonely in the end!

You Choose

Be heard?
or
Be ignored?

If you MELTDOWN,
others stop listening to you!

If you USE YOUR WORDS,
others hear what you want to do!

You Choose

Get done fast?

or

Take forever?

If you stay ON TASK,
your work is done fast!

If you DAYDREAM or DAWDLE,
you will finish last!

You Choose

Relaxed?

or

Worried?

If you act BRAVE,
Fewer worries will you know!

If you act FEARFUL,
your worries will grow and grow!

St**o**p • **T**hi**n**k • **C**hoose

***BEFORE* you DO**

to make good consequences

happen for you!

About the Author
Dr. Mary Ann Frost

Dr. Mary Ann Frost graduated Summa cum Laude from Purdue University with a B.A. in Psychology; earned an M.A. from Bowling Green State University; and completed a Doctorate in Counseling & Mental Health with a focus on Counseling Psychology and Family Therapy at the University of Toledo. She received family therapy training at the Accademia di Psicoterapia della Famiglia in Rome, Italy. She is Board Certified in Professional Counseling and Relationship Counseling.

She has a private practice in psychotherapy and life coaching which she approaches from an Adlerian perspective. She lives with her family in Palm Harbor, Florida, in a home filled with reminders of the many Powerful Journeys in her life.

About the Illustrator
Nila SM Soriano
cesnil@yahoo.com

Nila San Miguel Soriano has been a freelance artist for almost twenty years. She earned her Bachelor in Fine Arts degree at the University of Santo Tomas, Manila, Philippines. In 1984, she immigrated to the US and settled in St. Petersburg, Florida with her husband and three young children. Shortly after, she started a career in graphic arts. While working for different companies as a graphic designer, she started to take on freelance jobs as an illustrator, and soon decided to leave the workforce to become a full-time freelancer.

Over the years, she has developed different illustration styles. She believes that every project is unique and distinct style is necessary to support the intended message of the author.

Visit us at: www.mypowerfuljourneys.com

Helpful hints for parents, teachers, and counselors:

This book was written to support children's understanding and skills as they learn to manage emotions, identify options, and make choices based on desirable consequences before they take action.

The consequence-choices in this book highlight five competencies or "mental muscles" that all children need to be successful in life: awareness, connect-ability skills, self-discipline, capability, and decision-ability skills. The goal is to help a child cool down and think, and then link the choices with the consequences.

You can help children develop their decision making skills by:
⇨ Reading and discussing this book with them.

⇨ Teaching the self-soothing behaviors described in the Stop section. These behaviors can be used to interrupt impulsive actions and cool down.

⇨ Encouraging each child to think out loud about their goals, the options available to them, and the consequences of each option.

⇨ Support children in identifying behaviors that lead to desired consequences.

CPSIA information can be obtained
at www.ICGtesting.com
Printed in the USA
BVHW021957100620
581241BV00002B/28